A Pictorial Guide

to

Saudi Ar

Oman, UAE, Yemen, Bahrain, Kuwait, Qatar

Siân Pritchard-Jones
Bob Gibbons

First edition: 04 April 2020; ISBN: 9798630922540
Published by Expedition World; www.expeditionworld.com; sianpj@hotmail.com

Front cover photo: Emarah Palace, Najran
Back cover photo: Wadi Qaraqir & Nizwa mosque
Title page photo: Shaqra entrance gate

A Pictorial Guide
to
Saudi Arabia

Oman, UAE, Yemen, Bahrain, Kuwait, Qatar

Siân Pritchard-Jones
Bob Gibbons

About the authors

Siân Pritchard-Jones and Bob Gibbons met in 1983, on a trek from Kashmir to Ladakh. By then Bob had already driven an ancient Land Rover from England to Kathmandu (in 1974), and overland trucks across Asia, Africa and South America. He had also lived in Kathmandu for two years, employed as a trekking company manager. Before they met, Siân worked in computer programming and systems analysis. Since they met they have been leading and organising treks in the Alps, Nepal and the Sahara, as well as driving a bus overland to Nepal. Journeys by a less ancient (only 31-year-old) Land Rover from England to South Africa provided the basis for several editions of the Bradt guide **Africa Overland**, including the sixth edition published in April 2014 and the seventh coming soon.

In 2007 they wrote the Cicerone guide to **Mount Kailash** and Western Tibet, as well updating the **Grand Canyon** guide. Their **Annapurna** trekking guide was first published by Cicerone in January 2013, with the 2nd edition in 2017. In 2015 they were in Nepal during the earthquakes and published **Earthquake Diaries: Nepal 2015**. A Pictorial Guide to the **Horn of Africa** (Djibouti, Eritrea, Ethiopia and Somaliland), **Australia: Red Centre Treks** and **In Search of the Green-Eyed Yellow Idol**, a 40-year travelogue & autobiography, are published by Expedition World. See also **Saudi Arabia**, **Chad Sahara**, **Ladakh**, **Lebanon** and **Karakoram K2 treks**.

For Himalayan Map House they are writing a new series of trekking guidebooks: **Himalayan Travel Guides**. **Kanchi's Tale** is a new series of books covering various expeditions as seen through the eyes of a young Nepalese mountain dog – an educational doggie travelogue!

See back page for titles so far published. All books are also available on Amazon worldwide.

Authors at Wabah Crater, Central Saudi Arabia

Please send your comments and updates to sianpj@hotmail.com

Acknowledgements

Thanks to Florent Egal for his help before our trip and for all his amazing efforts to produce a great, informative and inspirational website. See www.saudiarabiatourismguide.com

Special thanks to Axel Michaelowa from Switzerland for his enthusiasm and for the background literature he has collated from many sources.

Many thanks to Mohammad Al-Anazi (Executive Director of Al Ula Cooperative Tourism Association and official licensed tour guide) for organising our 4x4 trip to Jibal al-Rukkab and for always being there on WhatsApp when we had a question about the rest of the country.

And lastly, thanks to any readers who venture to Arabia soon.

Contents

Preface

There are many familiar travel destinations across the world that inspire would-be adventurers and tourists. In this series of Pictorial Guides, the countries are globally well known, but not all the destinations are familiar to travellers. Saudi Arabia is the main focus of this guide, having just opened to tourism. Oman has blossomed into a great destination for interested visitors. The UAE, including Dubai, is a very popular stopover destination, but sadly Yemen will be off-limits and unknown for some time. Bahrain, Kuwait and Qatar have become popular transit points for travellers and host enough interest for a few days. Across the region, the people are welcoming, charming and helpful.

Anyone with a sense of adventure and keen to get to know some unfamiliar places of the world should not hesitate to make a journey.

It's a dangerous business, Frodo, going out your door. You step on to the road, and if you don't keep your feet, there's no knowing where you might be swept off to.
***The Lord of the Rings,* J R R Tolkien**

Introduction

This pictorial guide is essentially an introduction to Saudi Arabia, after its long isolation from the wider world. It also briefly encapsulates the other three main countries of Arabia, with token references to the other three smaller domains of the region. Basic outline information is provided, but for more in-depth information, see various designated guidebooks to the region.

The Arabian Peninsula is one of the most diverse parts of the greater Middle East. The four main countries of the region – Saudi Arabia, Yemen, Oman and the United Arab Emirates – are much more than desert. The region hosts high mountains, fertile plateaux, vast areas of sand dunes, tranquil canyons, enthralling escarpments, barren scrub, life-giving rivers and harsh desert plains. As diverse as the geography are the people who call this place home. Highland farmers, date cultivators, Bedouin camel herders, semi-nomadic seasonal herders, wild-eyed tribal clans, modern businessmen, traditional and modern well-covered women, and well-heeled elites are all found here. Parts of the region have rapidly growing economies, while others owe much of their prosperity to foreign intervention. There is also the misery of human tragedy and war.

Arabia is a wild and rugged region, where some of nature's most powerful actions are creating ghostly new terrain, splitting a continent and painting an inhospitable landscape in stupendously vivid colours. It's a little-known fact that much of Western Saudi Arabia is a vast volcanic region of lava fields and once-active volcanoes. The deserts may have been semi-tamed by wide multi-lane highways, but there are still remote places where hidden canyons, contorted plateaux and isolated wadis remain almost in solitude.

Saudi Arabia This is by far the largest country, but paradoxically it is also the least known. Its borders only opened to tourism in late 2019, yet already a small stream of adventurers have discovered places, sights and history that few could have imagined. Modernity may mask some of its treasures, but delve into the little-known cities dotted around the vast deserts, and amazing places are to be found. There are high mountains and plateaux, picture-postcard canyons, deep defiles, palm-clad paradises in hidden wadis, vast tracts of wild dunes and endless empty plains disturbed only by the wind. It's no surprise to find a country steeped in history – it is, after all, the birthplace of a world religion, but the variety and number of archaeological and historic sites is staggering. Saudi Arabia is on the cusp of being discovered by more than just a few invited engineers, guest workers and pilgrims.

Oman Not quite as well known as the UAE, Oman is a gem, little explored and waiting to show off its lesser-known side. It too has rugged mountains, historic sites and great areas of wilderness. The deserts here are as alluring as any in the world – salt pans, dunes, hidden canyons and a rugged coastline hardly noticed by anyone. Modernity is all around, but so is ancient culture and traditional heritage. Oman is an amazing place to discover.

United Arab Emirates (UAE) In stark contrast to Saudi Arabia, the UAE has been open to the world for years. Indeed, it is a modern-day crossroads of the world, with trade, tourism, international flight connections and many more new sectors of commerce. Away from the conurbations of the Gulf coast, the geography is little different from the eastern reaches of Saudi Arabia; dunes and sandy plains fan out from a few rugged mountains. Modern agriculture has spawned from the underground water and the few traditional oases.

Yemen The day will surely come eventually when this incredible country is at peace – enough for a trickle of travellers to rediscover what is not widely known. Few have been able to visit the Hadramawt region that was once locked away by the regime of the former South Yemen, but some (like us) were lucky to explore the northern part of the country. We found the 'real' Arabia in its walled mud cities, animated souks, dramatic escarpments, remote deserts and historic remains. It's a very tribal society, one that few will ever understand, but should the day ever come when it's safe, many will make tracks for this little-known corner of Arabia.

Bahrain, Kuwait and Qatar These countries are well-known for their oil wealth, modern cities and lifestyles. Though not really noted for their scenery, there are small desert retreats. Most visitors come as a stopover for a few days to experience the ambience and atmosphere of the Gulf region.

This pictorial guide aims to open a new window on Saudi Arabia since its sudden opening to tourism in late 2019. Arabia is not only Saudi Arabia, but a fascinating mix of other no-less-captivating states. Oman, UAE, Yemen, Bahrain, Kuwait and Qatar are included in outline for a wider perspective.

General information

Getting there
The main airlines serving the region are Saudi Arabian Airlines (Saudia), Emirates, Etihad, Oman Air, Gulf Air, Kuwait Airways and Qatar Airways, plus Middle Eastern carriers Turkish, Egypt Air, Jordanian and Middle East Airlines, plus most of the major European carriers. In addition there are other so-called budget airlines like Air Arabia, FlyDubai, Salaam Air, Jazeera Airways, Flynas, Nesma Airlines and FlyaDeal.

Landscapes
For a region with so much desert, Arabia has a surprising variety of landscapes, as mentioned above. The southern Asir mountains rise to almost 3000m. The Sarawat range runs inland along the Red Sea down through Yemen to Aden, with wild and remote places where few ever venture. Further inland are wild contorted canyonlands, and yet further east are vast lava fields (harrats) with dormant volcanoes and volcanic cones. The central and eastern region, including the UAE and Oman, is a vast sandy tract of low dunes, plains and outcrops. Finally, the vast area of the south and southeast is filled by the wastes of the Rub al-Khali – The Empty Quarter.

Climate

The best season to visit is undoubtedly from November to early April, when temperatures are cooler. In the desert and the north it can be surprisingly cold at night. Temperatures are hotter in the south; sandstorms are common in spring as the desert heats up. The southern Asir mountains can see snow on the highest peaks in winter, but the altitude ameliorates the heat for much longer than elsewhere. In the east, the searing temperatures last from April through to late November; it can be unbearable in summer, with temperatures up to 50°C. Only the coastal areas of Oman get a respite, with shoreline breezes at times.

Money matters

Changing money is not very easy in Saudi Arabia, except at the main airports. UAE has more exchange bureaux and Oman has some, but most visitors now use ATMs. Hotels change cash, but not at very good rates.

Religion

Across Arabia the religion is overwhelmingly Islam. Most of the countries are predominantly Sunni Muslim, with small communities of Shia. Bahrain has populations observing both. Yemen has sizeable groups of Ismailis, as well as both main sects of Islam. Pockets of Christians are rare, and most of the Jewish communities left years ago. That said, although most of the great influx of migrant workers are Muslim, a few are not.

Health and safety

Healthwise the countries have mostly good modern hospitals, although visitors will need insurance. Saudi Arabia imposes extra fees for health insurance when issuing the e-visa. The countries are subject to malaria, but the vast desert areas mean it's more limited to low, hotter coastal areas. Check with medical experts, though, as things are changing with global warming. Food hygiene is generally good at hotels and popular restaurants. Beware any empty lunchtime spots. All of the Arabian Peninsula, apart from Yemen and the border areas adjacent to it, are by most standards very safe to visit. Crime is minimal and, apart from the chance of a significant terrorist incident, few visitors feel threatened.

Visas

Saudi Arabia

Visas are required for all except some of the Gulf Co Operation States. Tourist e-visas are available online and, once the questions have been filled in correctly, there should not be a problem. A paper copy of the visa should be printed. In addition to the visa cost, there is an additional fee for mandatory basic medical care. See www.saudiarabiavisa.com

Oman

The e-visa for Oman is available online. Check at www.omanvisaonline.org

United Arab Emirates

Many nationals do not require a visa to enter the country. Check before any travel plans are finalised.

Yemen

Visas for entry to the Hadramawt are, in theory, available from Oman, but it would be pretty mad to try this option even if it does still operate.

Bahrain

Visas are available on arrival and may require proof of a ticket to leave the country.

Kuwait

The e-visa for Kuwait is available online. Some nationalities can get a visa on arrival. Check at www.evisa.moi.gov.kw

Qatar

Visas are available on entry, with an onward ticket. The ongoing issues between the Gulf communities and Qatar had not been resolved at the time of publication.

Travelling around

Drive on the right. Most roads in Saudi Arabia are dual carriageways, often with three lanes in each direction. Country roads are sealed, sometimes wide and occasionally narrower. Driving standards in cities are, shall we say, impatient. No one uses an indicator and driving in towns is nerve-racking, with lane discipline non-existent. Car hire is good value when booked beforehand with the well-known companies; fuel is very cheap. Be sure to get the full insurance locally. Long-distance buses link most major towns and are operated by SAPTCO. There are two train lines: the lines between Jeddah, Makkah and Madinah are for the Hajj and Umrah pilgrims. The other line between Riyadh, Buraydah, Ha'il and Al Jawf is useful for those without wheels. Elsewhere across the Gulf and Oman, roads are excellent. Most major centres are linked by buses. In towns and for some longer trips, there are taxis.

Budgeting

Saudi Arabia need not be prohibitively expensive for a longer independent stay. Hotels with large family-style apartments predominate, some with a basic kitchen included. Prices range from basic rooms for SR90 (US$25) to SR250 (US$60), with many around SR150 or so. The apartment-style places rarely provide towels and toiletries. Hotels provide more items, but not always. See the usual booking sites for ideas. Camping is not forbidden, but it's not that easy to find suitable places. Weekends 'getting back to nature' by locals and expats is quite popular, with their big 4X4s, cooking gear and basic shelters. Food from the many supermarkets and corner shops is varied, cheap and sustaining. Eating out is mainly in fast food places or, rarely, expensive hotel restaurants.

The Gulf States and Oman are similar in costs, with the UAE having more choice and a wider price range in general.

Latest news

Check before travel to the region for the latest updates. Saudi Arabia is changing fast as it gears up for the next winter season.

9

Map of Arabia

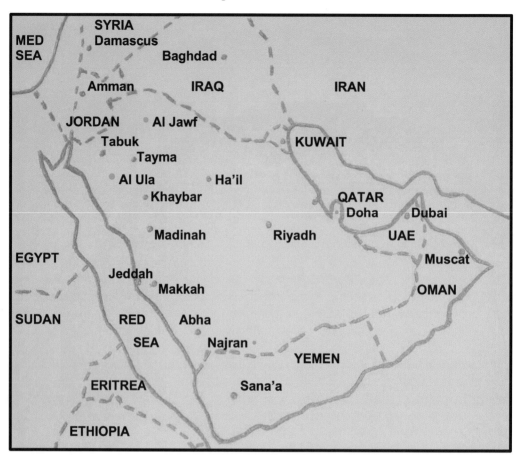

Old Jeddah backstreet – Was this once a hire car?

Saudi Arabia

The old historic Saudi Arabia – mud settlements like old Shaqra

And the ultra-modern Saudi Arabia – downtown Riyadh

Outline information

Introduction

Saudi Arabia, for so long an enigma to the rest of the world has finally opened its doors to tourism and is sure to be a popular destination. Little is generally known about the places to be visited, apart from the holy shrines of Islam, Makkah and Madinah. In fact the country is brimming with all manner of sights: historic archaeological sites including forts and ancient cities, prehistoric rock art and modern cultural attractions. The geography is also much more diverse than might be imagined. Apart from the deserts, which are interspersed with dunes, rocky plateaux and vast plains, there are hidden oases, deep canyons, amazing outcrops and mountains. The coasts are sure to attract divers and, in some designated areas in future, traditional sun-seekers.

Highlights

Saudi Arabia is a vast country and most visitors with limited time will have to decide on their priorities. The area of the country north and northwest of Jeddah and Riyadh holds so many amazing sights. Heading north from Jeddah, itself a fascinating window on the country with its old city of tower houses in Al Balad, the choices are varied. Most will head via Madinah (ring road) to the enchanting ancient oasis of Khaybar, with its ancient mud cities and nearby White Volcanoes. The top destination in the country is Al Ula and the Nabatean tombs of Mada'in Salih. The setting is fantastic, with amazing cliffs and outcrops in all directions. The tombs are, so far, a little-known treasure – after Petra, this was the second most important city of the long-lost Nabatean civilisation.

Continuing north, there is a choice between the small isolated oasis of Tayma, with its wells and palace, or the wild highlands that shelter the palm-fringed paradise of the Wadi Qaraqir canyon, the hard-to-reach Shaq canyon and some impressive 'Monument Valley' style ridges and outcrops. Tabuk is the northern centre and a good base for exploring the Jebal Hisma canyons, the ancient historic sites linked to the biblical story of Moses at Maqna and the Tayeb al-Ism gorge. Also here, near Al Bada, are some further Nabatean remains at Madyan.

Riyadh hides its history, but the Masmak Fort and ancient Diriyah are superb; enough interest for a day or two. Northwest of Riyadh are the amazing mud cities of Shaqra, Ushaiger, Mithnab and Al Ghat. The ancient stone fort at Fayd was once a stopover for the caravans of traders and pilgrims between Baghdad and Makkah. Continuing northeast, the modern highway reaches Ha'il, where historic forts remain. The premier rock art site of Jubbah is a must for all; from there the rolling dunes of the Nefud desert have been tamed by modern tarmac leading to Al Jawf. Here the superb Qasr Marid castle dominates an ancient city with mosques and atmospheric remains. Nearby in Sakaka the fort of Qasr Zab'al is another impressive site on the pilgrimage route from the Middle East.

Those seeking cooler retreats should head south into the Asir highlands. This upland area is surprisingly fertile and hosts a string of new residential towns and cities.

Set on the edge of the escarpment that drops thousands of metres to the Red Sea are the historic of towns of Zee al-Ayn and Rijal al-Ma.

If security improves, the gem of the south is Najran, where Yemeni-style mud tower houses still remain along with forts and ancient remains. Pretty soon adventurous visitors will be diving into the Empty Quarter to discover its alluring dunes and experience the solitude and silence of the desert nights. The starry desert skies are magical – a soothing antidote to the frenetic modern life.

Capital
Ar Riyadh (Riyadh)

Language
Arabic, but in towns English is widely understood.

International telephone code
+966

Currency and rate
Saudi Arabian Rial (SAR); US$1 = SAR3.75 (currently fixed)

Where to stay

Jeddah
For a first couple of days the **Red Sea Palace** near the old city is ideal. With deals, it starts at around US50 per night dbls. Nearby is the **Albaia Hotel** for a bit less. Breakfast, which is superb, is extra. Near the airport is the **Garden Palace**. Jeddah does not have many budget hotels and the vast nature of the suburbs means it's not very practical to seek out places miles from the centre.

Riyadh
Most hotels in Riyadh are expensive, so check on the usual booking sites in advance for deals. Try a couple of hotels near the Avenue Mall. The Almakan 105 cost SAR180, the Al Muhaideb SAR250. The excellent Lulu supermarket in Avenue Mall has an amazing choice of food items, plus good takeaways. Those returning hire cars might try the Almakan 103 only 18km from the airport.

Madinah
Although non-Muslims cannot enter the sacred Haram area of the inner city, there are hotels outside the restricted area close to the ring roads. Try the **Golden Address** Hotel, or the **Sobob** (Sohab or Sahab) on Al Jameaat Road, SR150 for a good room. Next door is the green Hotel **Diyar el Sidik,** no sign in English, rooms SR150. Close to the roundabout nearby is **Al Badaia**.

Khaybar
There's a very limited choice, so check on the booking sites or drive around till you find somewhere. A cheapish option is te **El Farasi** north en route to the old citadel mud cities.

Al Ula

Al Ula is the top tourist destination and in season prices are ridiculously high. Initially try the hotels on the south side before town. Elsewhere there are the more moderate **Nasem Al Atheb Camp**, and thus far the cheapest **Aistirahat-Al Sahab** north of the Winter Park beyond Ekma. **Mada'in Salih** has no accommodation and entry depends on the bus system to the site from the Winter Park. Those with 4X4s can camp near Elephant Rock. Others could head north and east towards Al Jaharah, where desert camping looks possible.

Tabuk

Tabuk has a good choice, bookable on the usual websites. near the northern ring road are several excellent value **Al Eairy** apartments, from SR85.

Al Bada

Finding the one or two apartment options is not easy, but the rooms are fine for a night or two. There is supposed to be a similar place in Maqna, but nothing at Tayeb al-Ism. Down the coast the NASCO diving hotel is good but very pricey.

Duba

Qasr Al Balagha is great option for a reasonable price for what is on offer SR200+. Parking is easy and there are fast food outlets and a supermarket across the road. Another hotel nearby is the **Tal Al Sahel**.

Tayma

The Hotel **Jewel Places** is a good option in the western area, but it's not marked in English, so ask around.

Shaqra and Ushaiger

In Shaqra the **Hotel Asfar Suites** on the southwest side is excellent. Cheaper places are close by.

Ha'il

On the western side before the road to Jubbah is the quiet **Raoum Inn** for just under SAR200.

Al Jawf

The **Admato Hotel** on the southwest side of Dumat al-Jandal is good value, with rooms from SR130–200. Parking is also good in a private courtyard.

Baljureshi

Try **Mera Houses** on the west side of town: Rooms from SR150 plus tax (SR10). Other places are the **Saf Hotel** on the way in and the **Baljureshi Palace** in town. The expensive **Swiss International Park Hotel** is on the road south out of town.

Abha

For a splurge try the **Azd Hotel** near Al Basta, along the wadi. Otherwise drive out uphill on the road to Rijal al-Ma to find the **La Fontaine Sarat Abha** with rooms for SR130–150.

Najran

Off-limits as far as most western governments' travel advice goes, Najran has the **Hyatt Najran**. It's not part of the well-known international chain, but for security and a good room, it's fine at SR270.

As Sulayyil

En route to Riyadh from Najran, Qaryat Al Faw and Wadi Ad Dawasir, the **Al Naif** on the west side of town is a great place with plenty of parking. Rooms SR150.

Dammam

Mostly catering to the oil industry, hotels in the east tend to be expensive. See booking websites.

Wadi Qaraqir region

The best bet here for some trekking is to camp; there is a quiet area north of Disah. Expect new accommodation here in the coming seasons. There is a basic hotel at Shigry above a fuel station.

Further information

To date the only comprehensive offering is **A Traveller's Guide to Saudi Arabia** by Siân Pritchard-Jones & Bob Gibbons, Expedition World 2020.

Things are changing: Young women out for a coffee in town

Meeting the people of Saudi Arabia

Above: Meeting the local people at **Café Taaleel at Qasr Za'bal, Sakaka**

Below: Friendly girls in Al Jawf & Guide at Mada'in Saleh

Above: The animated **bazaars of Al Balad**, historic Jeddah

Below: Helpful and knowledgeable storytellers (Rawi) 'girl' **guides at Dedan**
Ask permission before taking such photographs

Above: Domestic tourism – Rijal al-Ma
Below: Relaxing during a hot day

Ladies out shopping along **the Corniche** in Jeddah

Above: Meeting the people of **Abu As Su'ud** near Najran

Below: Friendly man and girl at **Bir Hima** wells

Above: Lunch time in **Abha**

Below: Lunch time at the **White & Black Volcanoes** – local Bedouins graze their camels in the shallow craters

Lunch time in **Sakaka**

The good old days, 1974

On the road from Jordan to Tabuk 1974

Trouble in Riyadh

Saudi desert 1974: It ain't half hot mum!

Jeddah – a gateway to Saudi Arabia

Historic Jeddah – Al Balad area.
Tower house, Shafi mosque & art museum

Traditional tower house in **Al Balad**, the famous Café Magad

Local people, the covered bazaar, shopping in **Al Balad, Juffali Mosque**

Riyadh – the capital

Masmak Fort

Downtown Riyadh

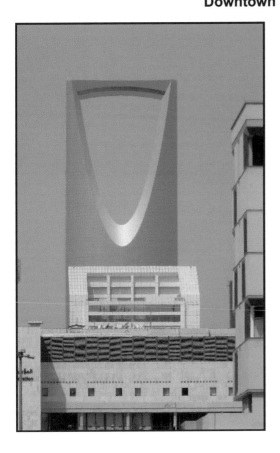

Riyadh Avenue Mall

Historic city of **Ad Diriryah** near Riyadh

Madinah

Haram area forbidden to non-Muslims

Hotel outside the Haram area

Mosque in the suburbs

Khaybar & the White Volcanoes

Above: Old Khaybar fort.   Below: citadel village

Jebel Bayda – the white volcano

Trekking near **Jebel Qidr** – the black volcano

Above: The desert is never dull, with lava fields, mountains and sand.
Below: The drive between Madinah and Al Ula

Al Ula

Panoramic view over **Al Ula**

Dedan outcrops

Elephant Rock

Dedan remains near Al Ula

Al Ula citadel and old city   **Outcrops** near town

Mada'in Salih

Above: Jebal Ithlib outcrops. **Below:** the **Diwan**

Some of the **131 tombs** at **Mada'in Salih**

Jibal al-Rukkab canyons

Amazing outcrops and **canyons** east of Mada'in Salih

Al Ragassan (Three Dancers) outcrops

Magic Mushroom outcrop north of Jibal al-Rukkab

Madakhil Arch north of Mada'in Salih

Fantastic scenery between **Al Ula** and **Wadi Qaraqir**

More amazing views en route to **Wadi Qaraqir** from **Al Ula**

Wadi Qaraqir canyon

One of the scenic surprises of Saudi Arabia – the **Wadi Qaraqir canyon** offers incredible views – a paradise of palm trees and cool waters

Trekking through **Wadi Qaraqir**

Gulf of Aqaba region

The little-known Nabatean tombs at **Madyan (Mu'gha'ir Shu'ayb)**

Wells of Moses (the twelve biblical springs) at **Maqna** on the Gulf of Aqaba opposite Mount Sinai in Egypt

The fabulous **Wadi Tayeb al-Ism** defile, said to be where Moses and his people arrived from Egypt after the 'exodus'; spot the tourists!

Duba harbour and port on the northern Red Sea

Lava fields and cinder cones of the **Harrat Lunayyir** near **Al Ays**

Trekking in Jibal Hisma

The fantastic dissected plateau of **Jibal Hisma** – a potential trekking area northwest of Tabuk, south of Wadi Rum in Jordan

Tabuk

Above: the **Hejaz** station & museum

Below: Tabuk historic **castle**

Tayma and Al Jawf region

Above: Tayma the ancient **Haddaj Wells**

Below: Dumat al-Jandal – old city and Omar Ibn al-Khattab mosque minaret

Above: Dumat al-Jandal, **Marid Fort**

Sakaka, **Qasr Za'bal Fort** & **Sisra well**

Qasr Za'bal, **Taaleel Cafe** for superb food and coffee
A great place to meet the friendly local people

Northern Nefud desert

Jubbah Rock Art site

Jubbah is possibly the premier site in Saudi Arabia for
Rock Art that dates back to Neolithic times

Images seen at the Jubbah Rock Art site

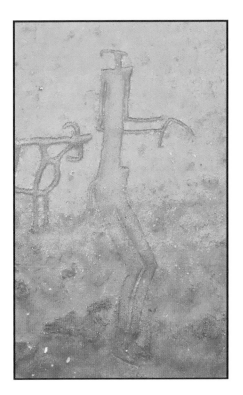

Ha'il

The modern city of **Ha'il** hides some historic gems – the **A'Arif Fort** is one that offers a great panoramic view over the modern city

Above: Qishlah Fort in Ha'il centre

Below: Laget Lelmedi Athr **Museum** in Ha'il

Above: The **Fort at Fayd** – a staging post on the pilgrim and trade routes between Baghdad with Makkah and Madinah

Below: Al Ghat another settlement of the pilgrim route

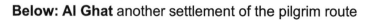

Above & below: Al Ghat historic settlement

Camels in the desert between **Buraydah and Al Ghat**

Ushaiger and Shaqra mud cities

Above: Ushaiger Palace and **below:** Typical city alleyway

In the old city streets of **Ushaiger** with its restored doorways

Above: Ushaiger oasis was a major stopover for trade caravans and pilgrims

Below: Fulaigiyeh mosque in **Ushaiger old city**

Above: Old mud settlement of Shaqra

Below: Al Subaia palace in old Shaqra

Above: the deep **Shaqra wells, Below: Al Dhwaihy** Fort

Red dunes between Shaqra and Riyadh

Above: Typical **Bedouin** tent

Below: Wabah Crater southeast of Madinah

Makkah and Taif

Above: Road sign on the **Makkah** southern ring road

Below: Taif Shubra Palace

Southern regions

The **Asir Mountains** and **Escarpment** form a high range up to nearly 3000m
inland from the Red Sea, with fertile uplands and settlements

Typical view of the **Asir Escarpment** along the **Southern Red Sea**

The picturesque stone-built village of **Zee al-Ayn** is hidden
on the edge of the escarpment

Historic **watch tower** and traditional **houses** in the **Asir**

Above: **Asir stone tower house** and **Hamadrayas baboons**,
a common sight in the mountains

Below: The **Escarpmen**t runs for over 600km from south of Jeddah to the Yemen border. A similar escarpment is seen in Eritrea across the Red Sea

Abha City

Above: Mosque in **Abha**, one of many in this modern southern city

Below: The modern classic-styled **Abha municipal buildings**

Above: Abha Asiri Museum and central mosque

Below: Typical Asiri architecture in **Al Basta** area of Abha

Above: Ottoman built bridge in Al Basta area of Abha

Below: Road down the **escarpment** to **Rijal al-Ma**

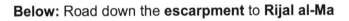

Rijal al-Ma

Above: Rijal al-Ma

Below: Rijal al-Ma **Museum house**

Above: Rijal al-Ma village & mosque **Below:** New teahouse

Local tourism – Selfies

Najran and the Far South

Above: Najran – Emarah Palace

Below: The old city remains of **Abu As Su'ud** west of Najran

Above: Najran **Al Aan Fort**

Below: Najran **Historic mud tower houses**

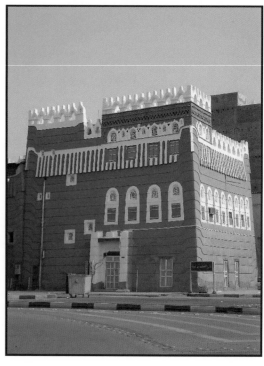

Najran: **Mud tower houses** – built in the typical Yemeni-style

Najran: Ancient pre-Islamic remains of **Ukhdood**

Warning:
Local travel agents in Abha recommend avoiding Najran for now until the war concludes. That is not to say anyone would be stopped on the way. Checkposts might stop tourists, but the official policy is unclear. Your travel insurance may not be valid. Those proposing to visit should clearly accept the risks, which are hard to assess. That said, approaching Najran from Wadi Ad Dawasir is a better option, as the route avoids the border road coming from Abha.

Check the various government travel advisory websites before a visit. The Houthis claim to have raided the Najran border areas as recently as June 2019, although reports are not verified.

Najran Emarah Palace

Najran Emarah Palace souk (Suq)

Najran city panorama at dusk

Above: Bir Hima wells near a premier **Rock Art** site

Below: Well at Hima – one of seven life-giving wells

The Empty Quarter

The **Rub al-Khali** (Empty Quarter) covers a vast region of the
south and southeast of Saudi Arabia.
North of Najran, the **Jebal Tuwayq escarpment** lies east of the road.

Camels were once the lifeblood of the Arabian deserts
– now it's a Toyota **4X4**

Uruk Bani Ma'arid Reserve

Luxury camping in the reserve

Qaryat Al Faw – historic oasis on the frankincense trade routes between Yemen and the Middle East

Cliffs en route to **As Sulayyil** between Najran and Riyadh

Above: Old city remains of **Layla** – a settlement on the western edge of the **Rub al-Khali**

Below: Layla old mosque

Above: Sunset on the Red Sea

Below: Sundown in Jeddah

Oman

Above: Muscat city gate

Below: Muscat Matruh Corniche and bay

Introduction
Oman was once also a restricted country, but since opening has developed a great tourism sector. Much of the country is desert, bordering the Rub al-Khali to the northwest, but along much of the coast there are mountainous areas rising from the Indian Ocean. Oman mixes its ancient heritage well with a modern, progressive outlook. Today Oman is a superb place to enjoy the ambiance of Arabia, along with a wide range of diverse desert experiences.

Highlights
The capital Muscat and its adjacent settlements, Matruh or Mutruh and Ruwi, have a picture-postcard setting on the ocean, with historic forts and lively markets. Closer to Muscat the peaks rise to over 3000m, with hidden canyons and small oases, accessed by some rugged roads. Inland is the historic and picturesque oasis of Nizwa, nestling below rugged mountains. Forts, some restored and others in ruins, dot the inland side of the mountains: places like Ibri, Jabrin and Buraimi.

In the southwest the region of Dhofar hosts the rare frankincense trees/plants in the uplands around Salalah. Most of the long Indian Ocean coast is unexplored, with wild rocky bays and windswept cliffs. The rolling dunes and dry salt pans of the northern deserts hide lost oases and a solitude that is so rare today.

Capital
Muscat

Language
Arabic, but in towns and cities English is widely understood.

International telephone code
+968

Currency and rate
Omani Rial (OMR); US$1 = OMR0.39

Where to stay
Oman and Muscat in particular is not generally a cheap location, but there are some mid-range and budget options. Check the usual booking websites for the latest offers.

Above: Muscat Matruh Corniche houses, Below: Matruh bazaar

Above: Muscat Matruh Corniche

Below: Inland is the verdant **Nizwa** oasis

Above: Nizwa fortress. **Below: Nizwa market** and **mosque**

Ancient remains of Ibri fort & Buraimi castle

Above: The historic **Jabrin Fort**

Below: Sunset on **Muscat Fort**

United Arab Emirates (UAE)

Above: Dubai – Sheikh Sayeed. Below: Dubai Souk & Creek waterfront

Introduction
The region of the UAE was once the domain of isolated fishermen and pearl divers, long before the discovery of oil in the 1930s. Today the staggering urbanisation along the coast and the ultra-modern skyline has transformed the region beyond recognition. For the last three decades an incredibly dynamic economic, cultural and progressive phase has made the United Arab Emirates a world crossroads.

Highlights
The natural wonders of the country are the rolling dunes of the hinterland in the south, along with a few verdant oases, like Liwa and the Musandam peninsula shared with Oman. As the UAE has worked to diversify its economy away from dependence on oil, the variety of sights and activities has expanded. The coast has seen some incredible developments for beach and leisure tourism.

As for the cities, the architectural wonders are amazing; Dubai is famed for its Burj Khalifa Tower. Dubai Creek hosts a small historic area, with the Dhow Museum, Sheikh Sayeed House and the old waterfront area. The souks and street markets are a magnet for all. Sharjah has its own restored historic area, as does Abu Dhabi to a degree.

Capital
Abu Dhabi, but each emirate has its own centre.

Language
Arabic, but in towns English is widely understood.

International telephone code
+971

Currency and rate
UAE Dirham (AED); US$1 = AED3.65

Transport
There are some long-distance buses that also cross to Oman and Saudi Arabia. Buses run from the airports and taxis are plentiful.

Where to stay
The three main centres, Dubai, Sharjah and Abu Dhabi, have many top range hotels; there are also mid-range and more affordable options that can be found on the usual websites. The cheaper establishments often cater to the migrant and business guests.

Above: Dubai Creek at sunset. **Below:** Mosque blue tiling

Dubai Dhow Museum

Above: museum in **Sharjah**

Below: mosque in **Sharjah**

Yemen

The Yemeni capital Sana'a has a large and amazing old city.
There were some atmospheric old quarters, picturesque gardens and
mud-built tower houses up to five storeys high.

Introduction
In the 1980s, Yemen was the Arabian country to visit to experience the traditional, cultural and natural wonders of the region. Sadly, those days are long gone. If peace and security ever return, the country has amazing assets to re-exploit, as can be seen from the photos here in this book.

Highlights
The capital Sana'a was a truly exotic city in the 1980s – a wonderful place to sink into the culture and atmosphere of Arabia. The old city was just amazing to visit, with mud tower houses, bustling souks and mysterious alleys. The countryside hosted hilltop fortified villages, amazing palaces, quiet rural villages and rugged mountain scenery. Taiz was a busy place and the Red Sea coast a humid and rural backwater, apart from the port of Hodeidah.

In the north the mud city of Sada'a could only have been dreamed of in a movie – the real Arabian Nights town. The east hosted the remains of the Queen of Sheba's temple, while in what was formerly South Yemen, the fabulous mud cities of the Hadramawt – Seiyun, Shibham and Tarim – remain unknown to outsiders. Whether Aden will ever be a tourist destination again is anyone's guess.

Capital
Sana'a

Language
Arabic, but in towns English was widely understood in the towns.

International telephone code
+967

Currency and rate
Yemeni Rial (YER); US$1 = YER250 and fluctuating

Transport
Intercity transport used to be by surprisingly modern, if mostly worn-out, long distance buses. Amazingly the Saudi bus company SAPTCO runs a service between Jeddah and Sana'a even today.

Where to stay
There were some good mid-range options (like the Sam City Hotel in Sana'a) but we have no information worth printing. The budget options were quite grim, some dormitory-style local places (funduqs).

Above: Bab-al-Yemen Gate

Below: Children scurry about **Old Sana'a**

Traditional mud-built tower houses in Sanaa

In the animated and colourful markets of **Old Sana'a**

Above: Sana'a merchant tower houses

Below: Sana'a city walls in the south

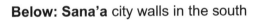

Highland view across Yemen, south to **Taiz**

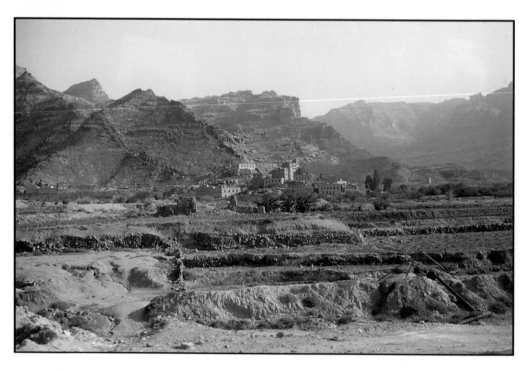

Descending the escarpment east to **Marib** and the **Hadramawt**

Above: Typical rural Yemeni hill villages near Sana'a, **Kawkaban**

Below: Shibham

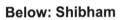

Above: Wadi Dhar Palace & below: Wadi Dhar valley

Above: The mountain town of **Taiz**. **Below: Hookah pipe shop**

Taiz at sunset

Above: Hodeidah port on the Red Sea
Below: Settlement on the coastal **Tihama plains**

Curious local girls

Above: Amarah en route north to Sada'a. **Below: Sada'a**

Sada'a: Ismaili mosque

The amazing superb mud architecture of **Sada'a** is
very similar to that seen in Najran, Saudi Arabia.
Before 1934 Najran was a semi-independent fiefdom of Yemen

Eastern Yemen: Old Marib village & Axumite remains

Typical sunset over Yemen

Bahrain, Kuwait and Qatar

Bahrain was once an island off the coast of Saudi Arabia until a new causeway linked it to the mainland. Long a trading port and fishing centre in the Gulf, it now has a very diverse population with people from differing cultural backgrounds. Bahrain these days is also a popular stopover in the region. **Kuwait** was once the domain of isolated fishermen and pearl divers. As with all the Gulf States, urbanisation and the impressive skyline have transformed the city beyond recognition. Apart from the disastrous war in 1990-91, the country has also grown for the last three decades to become a leading player in the region. **Qatar** stands on a small peninsula projecting into the shallow waters of the Gulf. It's not so long ago that its capital, Doha, was a sleepy, low-rise town. Today Qatar has become a new international crossroads, with ever-expanding facilities and a tourist sector.

Highlights

Bahrain – the main settlement **Al Manamah** has seen its fair share of modernisation from a low-rise, bustling town over the last forty years. **Kuwait City** was one of the first in the region to introduce some futuristic structures opened in the 1970s. Today the city has grown massively with modern malls, beautiful mosques and a skyline along the waterfront the equal of any in the region. A stroll along the corniche waterfront on the northern side is a favourite pastime at sunset as the heat of the day gives way to cool breezes. **Doha** in **Qatar** has made extraordinary efforts to regenerate some of its historic areas and to enhance the traditions of the country. The superb skyline along the waterfront is the certainly attractive and dynamic. Most visitors to Qatar stop over for a short time to enjoy the remodelled souk and enjoy the outdoor ambience of the street cafés.

Capitals

Al Manamah, Kuwait City and Doha

Language

Arabic, but in towns English is widely understood.

International telephone code

Bahrain +973, Kuwait +965 and Qatar +974

Currency and rate

The currencies, Bahrain Dinar (BHD), Kuwaiti Dinar (KWD) & Qatari Rial (QAR) are convertible.

Transport

In Bahrain most transport is by taxi. From Kuwait there are a few long-distance buses to Saudi Arabia. Most transport in Kuwait City and Doha is by taxi. Currently restrictions are in place for travel to neighbouring countries from Doha.

Where to stay

Comprehensive guidebooks and internet information are available for the Gulf countries. There are mostly expensive and mid-range options, with a few cheaper options in all the countries. See the usual booking websites for deals.

Bahrain – busy street in a sweltering **Al Manamah street**

Teatime is a daily ritual across **Arabia**

Above: Modern traditional-style buildings in Kuwait

Above: Kuwait Dhow harbour 1974

Above: Flying into **Kuwait City** 2020

Above: Doha harbour 2019
Below: Night musicians & street café at festival time

Night bazaar in Doha

Doha skyline at night

If you've enjoyed this book, or been inspired to find out more, please see our other books, in particular

Saudi Arabia: A Traveller's Guide --- **2020**
Horn of Africa: A Pictorial Guide --- **2020**
Africa Overland: A Pictorial Guide --- **2020**
Asia Overland: A Pictorial Guide --- **2020**

Bradt (www.bradtguides.com)
Africa Overland --- 2005, 2009, 2014, new edition due 2021

Cicerone (www.cicerone.co.uk)
The Mount Kailash Trek --- 2007
Annapurna: A Trekker's Guide --- 2013, 2016

Amazon / Kindle (www.amazon.com)
In Search of the Green-Eyed Yellow Idol --- 2015, 2016, 2019
(an autobiography)
Earthquake Diaries: Nepal 2015 --- 2015
The Horn of Africa: A Pictorial Guide --- 2016, 2020
Australia: Red Centre Treks --- 2016
Kanchi's Tale:
Kanchi goes to Makalu Base Camp --- 2017
Kanchi goes to the Tibesti, Chad --- 2017
Chad: Tibesti, Ennedi & Borkou --- 2017, 2020
Karakoram: The Highway of History --- 2018
Ladakh: A Land of Mystical Monasteries --- 2018
Lebanon: A Brief Guide --- 2019
Karakoram & K2 Concordia (trekking guide) --- 2019
Saudi Arabia: A Traveller's Guide --- 2020
Saudi Arabia: A Pictorial Guide --- 2020
Africa Overland: A Pictorial Guide --- 2020
South America: A Pictorial Guide --- 2020
Asia Overland: A Pictorial Guide --- 2020

Himalayan Map House (HMH) (www.himalayanmaphouse.com)
Himalayan Travel Guides (HTG) (www.himalayantravelguides.com)
& Amazon worldwide (www.amazon.com)
Manaslu & Tsum Valley --- 2013, 2016, 2019, 2020
Dolpo --- 2014, 2019; **Ganesh Himal** --- 2014
Langtang --- 2014, 2018, 2020; **Everest** --- 2014, 2018
Rolwaling --- 2015; **Mustang** --- 2016, 2019, 2020
Kanchenjunga --- 2017; **Makalu** --- 2017
West Nepal --- 2017; **Dhaulagiri** --- 2018
Nepal Himalaya --- 2015, 2017, 2019

Pilgrims (www.pilgrimsonlineshop.com)
Kathmandu: Valley of the Green-Eyed Yellow Idol --- 2005
Ladakh: Land of Magical Monasteries --- 2006
Kailash & Guge: Land of the Tantric Mountain --- 2006

Printed in Great Britain
by Amazon